BUILD A DUCK
AND OTHER GREAT
LEGO® IDEAS

Contents

Book breakdown

This book shows lots of inspiring model breakdowns to help you discover ideas and techniques for your own models, but the entire book is broken down, too. There are many different types of pages designed to help you build up your own amazing LEGO® world, section by section, model by model, brick by brick.

Colored bars, like the one below, run along the top of pages to let you know what kind of page you're reading.

Page number | Page type

Section name

Here are all the different types of pages you'll find in this book:

How to build

Watch one model develop from start to finish on these pages, with helpful building advice at every stage.

What else can you build?

Once you've seen how to build one model, discover different ways of using similar techniques and ideas in your own models.

Expanding your world

Don't stop now! Once you've built a few models, why not add more to your world? These pages give ideas for building extra models and scenery.

Builder secrets

Ssshh! These pages reveal insider tips for building challenging parts of models or functions. Master the techniques to wow your friends!

Showstoppers

These pages show off the biggest or most interesting ideas in this book. Look at them in detail and use the ideas to build your own showstopper models.

A cell phone

Follow the LEGO® spaceman minifigure, Tech 4, as he discovers a new dimension where everything is HUGE. Is that a massive black monolith, towering over Tech 4? No—it's a life-sized cell phone.

START HERE

You can also put smaller plates together—just make sure the pieces you place on top lock them together well!

1 Brick technology

To build a flat, rectangular device, start with a flat, rectangular building surface. A 6x12 plate makes a perfect base for a sleek, black cellular telephone.

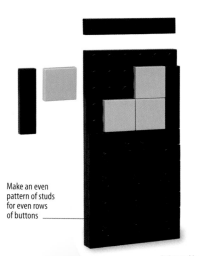

2 A thin layer

Keep your phone thin and streamlined by covering its flat areas with smooth tiles. Use single-studded jumper plates as connection points for buttons and other projecting details.

Make an even pattern of studs for even rows of buttons

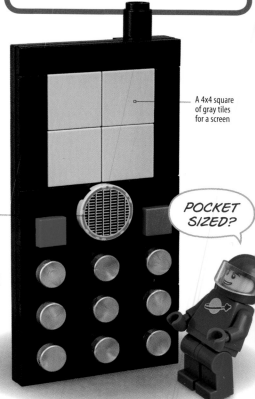

A 4x4 square of gray tiles for a screen

1x1 round brick plugged into a 2x2 plate with a round hole in its side

A printed 2x2 tile makes a good speaker—or use a pair of 1x2 grilles

POCKET SIZED?

3 Add the details

Now attach the pieces that will make this recognizable as a cell phone, such as buttons, a speaker, accept/reject buttons, and (if you want to go a little old-school) an antenna on top.

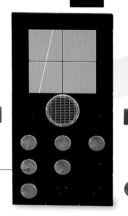

Use 1x1 round or square tiles for buttons

Colored tiles for accept/reject buttons

4 Beepity-boop

Your new phone is finished! Just don't accidentally mix it up with the real thing when you leave the house. Plastic bricks aren't good at making long-distance calls!

Technology

What other pocket-sized tech devices can you build using the same construction techniques as the cell phone? You could put together a calculator… or an MP3 player to store and play all of your favorite imaginary tunes.

MP3 PLAYER

Printed or stickered tiles for icons

WHAT'S NEXT?

Starting with the same kind of base plate as the cell phone, change around the details to create different devices.

2x2 round tile attached to a 2x2 plate

MP3 player

The key is to make your models look like what they're supposed to be with a few key details. Add screen icons and a round wheel to a music player, and its identity quickly becomes clear!

CALCULATOR

1x2 tiles are attached to 2x2 jumper plates

This 1x3 tile goes across two 2x2 jumper plates

Mix 1x1 and 1x2 tiles for different button shapes

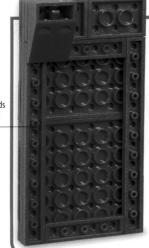

Extra layer of plates holds two 6x6 plates together in a 6x12 shape

Inverted angled bottom

2x3 studded top

Calculator

Try taking a look at the real thing before you build your LEGO brick version. The angled back and button layout make this calculator model seem extra-authentic.

Angled back

A row of inverted slopes on the back makes the calculator rest at an angle when set down.

Stationery

Behold these bizarre human tools that sit atop a vast and featureless plane. It seems to be a gigantic desk covered with writing and art supplies! Be inspired by everyday items like stationery to make something ordinary look extraordinary.

A 1x2 jumper plate makes the sharpener's blade

This eraser is made from just three pieces: a 1x4 brick and two 1x2 tiles

A 1x4 tile on top hides the studs

Pencil sharpener and eraser

Even a small handful of pieces can let you create stationery tools. Build them next to the real ones so you get the details and proportions right.

Ruler

Make a ruler by stacking up plates —white for the main body, and black for the lines. Altogether, this model is four studs across and 62 plates high!

HMM, I ALWAYS THOUGHT I WAS TALLER.

An arch on the lid and a dip on the box make a gap for a finger to flip it open

The lid opens on a row of three 1x2 snap-together hinges

REAR VIEW

Grilles attached to side studs mimic a bar code on the back

Crayon wrappers are identical stacks of tan and brown 1x1 round bricks and plates

Build colorful pieces into the walls of the box for decoration

Each end of the tube attaches to a round LEGO Technic connector pin

The two identical scissor halves are attached together by a pivoting, free-spinning LEGO® Technic connector pin.

Decorative swords can be found in LEGO® NINJAGO® sets

Crayon box

This box has a hinged lid that flips back to store the crayons inside. It can take a bit of practice to build one object that fits inside another, but the end result is worth it!

Scissors

These scissors can't cut, but they can open and close just like the real thing. Use straight LEGO Technic connectors and flexible tubes to make the handles, and LEGO sword pieces for the blades.

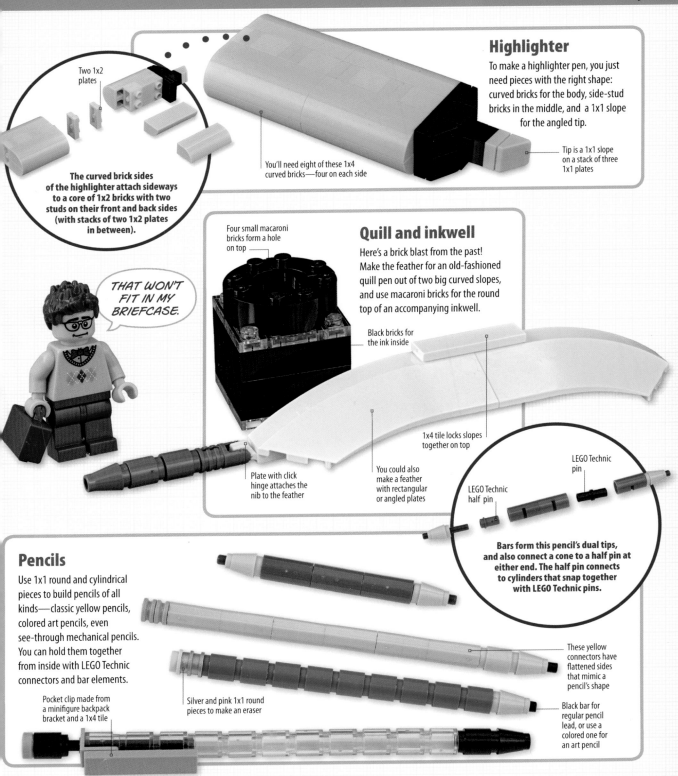

Highlighter

To make a highlighter pen, you just need pieces with the right shape: curved bricks for the body, side-stud bricks in the middle, and a 1x1 slope for the angled tip.

Two 1x2 plates

The curved brick sides of the highlighter attach sideways to a core of 1x2 bricks with two studs on their front and back sides (with stacks of two 1x2 plates in between).

You'll need eight of these 1x4 curved bricks—four on each side

Tip is a 1x1 slope on a stack of three 1x1 plates

THAT WON'T FIT IN MY BRIEFCASE.

Quill and inkwell

Here's a brick blast from the past! Make the feather for an old-fashioned quill pen out of two big curved slopes, and use macaroni bricks for the round top of an accompanying inkwell.

Four small macaroni bricks form a hole on top

Black bricks for the ink inside

1x4 tile locks slopes together on top

Plate with click hinge attaches the nib to the feather

You could also make a feather with rectangular or angled plates

LEGO Technic pin

LEGO Technic half pin

Bars form this pencil's dual tips, and also connect a cone to a half pin at either end. The half pin connects to cylinders that snap together with LEGO Technic pins.

Pencils

Use 1x1 round and cylindrical pieces to build pencils of all kinds—classic yellow pencils, colored art pencils, even see-through mechanical pencils. You can hold them together from inside with LEGO Technic connectors and bar elements.

Pocket clip made from a minifigure backpack bracket and a 1x4 tile

Silver and pink 1x1 round pieces to make an eraser

These yellow connectors have flattened sides that mimic a pencil's shape

Black bar for regular pencil lead, or use a colored one for an art pencil

WOOO HOOO!

I'M USED TO BEING WEIGHTLESS!

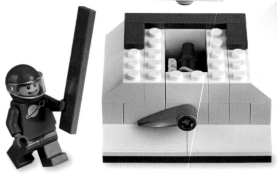

2x4 plate with three round holes

The heavier the weight on top, the more the dial moves

7 Final model

When the weighing plate's axle is pushed down, it pushes on the catch and pin, moving the dial on the outside of the scale. Let go, and it springs back up!

6 Pan attachment

Attach the plate with holes on the weighing pan attachment to the top of the scale, so that the weighing pan's cross axle rests on top of the catch-and-pin assembly inside, and cover the rest of the scale's top with smooth tiles.

Kitchen scale

Use your bricks to make a scale that really reacts to the weights you place on its platform. Tech 4 discovers that when you're the size of a LEGO minifigure, this human tool makes a great trampoline!

A strongly gripping bushing holds the gear in position

1 ▶ Inner workings

When creating a model with a built-in function, start by thinking about how the parts of the mechanism will work together. LEGO Technic pieces threaded onto a cross axle will move together when the axle turns.

Push a LEGO Technic pin with a cross-axle end into a catch with cross hole

Note this 1x1 brick with handle built into the wall next to the gap—it's important!

A 1x2 tile inside keeps the pin from getting stuck on the base's studs

2 ▶ Mechanism in place

Attach the mechanism's components to a base platform, like this 8x8 plate. Test the parts to make sure the cross axle rotates smoothly, and then start building up the scale's sides.

The brick with hole fits into this gap in the front wall

Large round plate for a weighing pan

5 ▶ A scale model

Build a weighing pan by attaching a 2x2 round brick underneath a large plate. Push a cross axle into the hole in the center of the 2x2 brick, and thread its other end through a tile with a hole and a plate with holes. Push a half bushing onto the end of the axle so it won't pop back out.

3 ▶ Dial it up

To make the scale's dial, slide a short LEGO Technic cross axle through a 1x2 brick with a round hole. Connect a small half gear on one side, and a LEGO Technic tooth piece on the other.

The elastic band pulls the catch and pin upwards

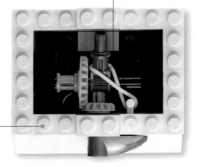

4 ▶ Elastic power

To give your scale a springy resistance when its top is pushed down, take a LEGO elastic band and give it a twist in the middle. Loop one end over the handle of a brick with handle in the wall, and the other over the LEGO Technic catch and pin attached to the central cross axle.

Side walls keep the main axle from sliding back and forth

Bathroom

Tech 4 finds himself inside a white, tiled chamber full of immense porcelain sculptures. Could this be the cavernous bathroom of some giant creature? What can you build from your own human bathroom?

FANCY A DIP?

Beak is an orange curved slope

Round 1x1 tile eyes attached to 1x1 bricks with side studs

Wings built around a 2x4 plate that sticks out on both sides of the body

Rubber ducky

Quack! Quack! Get out your yellow bricks and build yourself a life-sized rubber ducky model. This bathtime favorite uses slope bricks and tiles to create its smooth, studs-free shape. Build the head first, then construct the body from the base up.

WHO'S THAT HANDSOME CHAP?

Build the reflection out of one-stud-wide bricks and tiles

THAT FACE LOOKS VERY FAMILIAR.

Drawer handles are LEGO Technic balls attached to 1x2 bricks with holes using LEGO Technic pins

Shaving mirror

Who's that in the reflection of this tilting mirror? It's whoever you want it to be! Use your LEGO pieces mosaic-style to make up a funny face, or even build a bricky version of yourself.

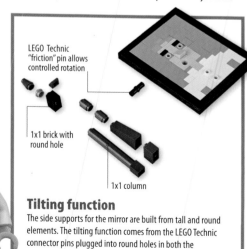

LEGO Technic "friction" pin allows controlled rotation

1x1 brick with round hole

1x1 column

Tilting function

The side supports for the mirror are built from tall and round elements. The tilting function comes from the LEGO Technic connector pins plugged into round holes in both the supports and the mirror frame.

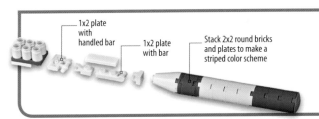

Bristles made from 1x1
round bricks on a 2x6 plate

Toothbrush

You could make a simple toothbrush
out of regular LEGO bricks, but this
one is a bit more stylish! Use 2x2
round elements for the handle, and
clip-and-bar hinges for an angled neck.

1x2 plate
with
handled bar

1x2 plate
with bar

Stack 2x2 round bricks
and plates to make a
striped color scheme

Flexible neck

The neck of the toothbrush is made
by locking a plate with bar and
a plate with clip together with
a tile on top. They attach to a clip
on the handle and a bar on the head.

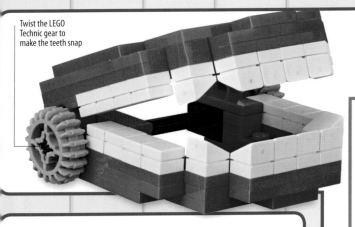

Twist the LEGO
Technic gear to
make the teeth snap

Dentures

It looks like someone has left a set of false teeth on the sink…or is
this a pair of chattering joke teeth? Use tiles and 1x1 slopes to make a
mouthful of shiny white teeth, with a turning gear to make them move!

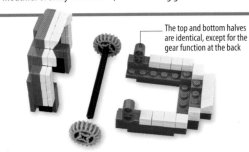

The top and bottom halves
are identical, except for the
gear function at the back

Biting function

A LEGO Technic cross axle goes through pieces with round holes on the
lower jaw, and bricks with cross-shaped holes on the upper jaw.

Comb

Use one-stud-wide pieces to build the flat handle of a comb. A row of
LEGO antennae makes a great line of long, thin teeth! With even more
antennae, you could use the same techniques to build a hairbrush, too.

Stack up slopes and bricks to
make the handle extensions
around the teeth

A 1x6 inverted curved
slope holds the end of the
comb together.

Antennae attach to the
studs of a long plate

Science kit

Now here's something that Tech 4 recognizes, even when the tools and equipment are huge. Somebody in this enormous house likes SCIENCE! Build life-sized equipment for your own LEGO brick scientific laboratory.

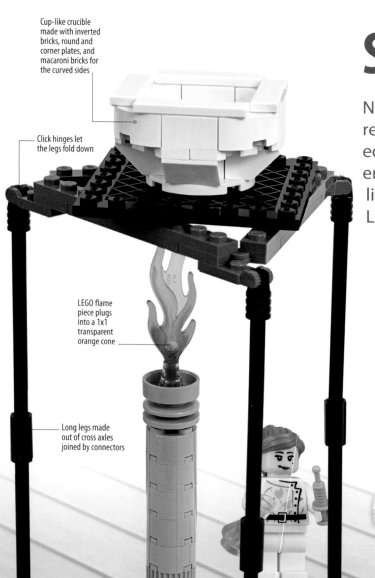

Cup-like crucible made with inverted bricks, round and corner plates, and macaroni bricks for the curved sides

Click hinges let the legs fold down

LEGO flame piece plugs into a 1x1 transparent orange cone

Long legs made out of cross axles joined by connectors

Lab equipment

What basic equipment might you find in a real-life lab? Here are some ideas: a flaming Bunsen burner, a tall tripod, a safety mat, and a heat-resistant crucible that sits on a gauze mat for heating up experiments.

Use brown and black tiles to make scorch marks

The mat is made from tiles on top of a large square plate

Broken Bunsen

The tall, thin main body of the Bunsen burner is a stack of 2x2 round bricks. One or more LEGO Technic cross axles pushed through the holes in the center of the pieces strengthen it from the inside.

The gas supply hose plugs onto a 2x2 brick with side pin

Tongs

Handle your LEGO experiments with care by using a set of tongs to move your test tubes around the lab. Thanks to the clever use of a rubber band, this full-sized model works just like the real thing!

Arch elements create a curved grip to safely hold cylindrical test tubes

Long curved slopes for the handles

Rubber band makes sure tubes can be held firmly

Tiles for a flush, smooth surface

Get a grip

Angle plate brackets and inverted angle plates attach angled plates to the sides of the tongs. The angled plates provide studs to hold the small elastic band in position.

Attach angled plates to both sides of each half

Thermometer and pipette

Create smaller tools for your LEGO lab, too. Make a thermometer by alternating 1x1 round bricks and 1x1 round plates, with a LEGO Technic ball at the bottom. For a measuring pipette, plug a bar into a stack of 1x1 round bricks for the thin tip, and build a squeezing bulb with a 2x2 radar dish, cone, and dome.

A small LEGO Technic cross axle holds this cone and dome together

PIPETTE

THERMOMETER

Red pieces indicate temperature

Test tubes

Build see-through test tubes out of clear round pieces, with colored elements for the mysterious chemicals bubbling and swirling inside. Make different colors and fluid levels for variety, and don't forget a rack to hold them upright!

Clear wheels for rims

Tubes are upside-down stacks of transparent 2x2 round bricks

This cross-axle connection lets the top and bottom ends of the stopper point in opposite directions

Use domes in matching colors for the bases

Replace a clear brick with a solid-colored one for the part of the stopper that's inside the tube

Rubber stopper

The stopper's top is a stack of two 2x2 round plates and a round tile, attached to a LEGO Technic cross axle pushed through the center hole of the wheel rim.

Try mixing different colors or adding detail pieces at the top to build chemical reactions into your tubes!

A banana

That was a close scrape! Tech 4 isn't sure what he just escaped from, but this looks like a much safer place to explore. In fact, it smells delicious…if a little over-ripe. Build life-sized food with your LEGO bricks, starting with a partly blackened banana!

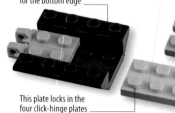

START HERE

This 4x4 sloped wedge piece provides the perfect curve for the bottom edge

This plate locks in the four click-hinge plates

1 ▶ **Round the bend**

Begin with one of the two middle sections of the banana. Because the model will be made up of jointed segments to give it a realistic curve, place click-hinge plates at both ends.

Use bricks for solid-color sections, or plates to make spots and patterns

2 ▶ **Shades of ripeness**

A perfectly ripe banana is all yellow, but this one may have gone off a bit! As you build up this body section with yellow bricks and plates, sprinkle in a few black ones to show age.

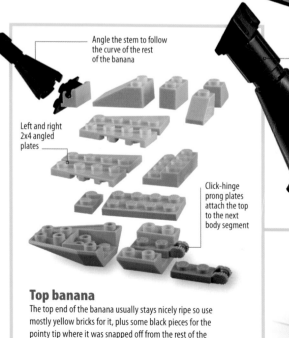

Angle the stem to follow the curve of the rest of the banana

Left and right 2x4 angled plates

Click-hinge prong plates attach the top to the next body segment

The stem is a 2x2 cone, 1x1 round brick, and 1x1 slope, attached to the tip with a snap-together hinge

AM I DREAMING?

Top banana

The top end of the banana usually stays nicely ripe so use mostly yellow bricks for it, plus some black pieces for the pointy tip where it was snapped off from the rest of the bunch. Underneath are inverted, sloped wedge pieces, while slopes and angled plates give it shape on top.

3 ▶ Finish the segment

Build the top of the banana segment with slope bricks, mirroring the shape of the angled piece underneath. Next, make another section with the same shape, but choose a different pattern of yellow and black pieces.

Use 2x2 or 1x2 slopes, depending on how big you want each block of color to be

Build the banana's core out of tan or white bricks, and then remove some of the yellow outer pieces to "peel" it!

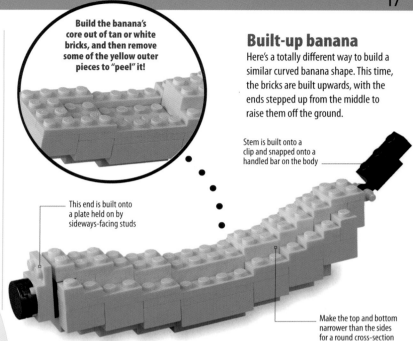

Built-up banana

Here's a totally different way to build a similar curved banana shape. This time, the bricks are built upwards, with the ends stepped up from the middle to raise them off the ground.

Stem is built onto a clip and snapped onto a handled bar on the body

This end is built onto a plate held on by sideways-facing studs

Make the top and bottom narrower than the sides for a round cross-section

4 ▶ Creativity with a curve

Once you've made another body section, assemble the two ends too (see the breakdowns of those to find out how), then combine the pieces into one amazing banana! By placing the click hinges near the bottom of each segment, you can bend them just enough to make a curved shape.

The second section is closer to the all-black end, so it has more black pieces than the first one

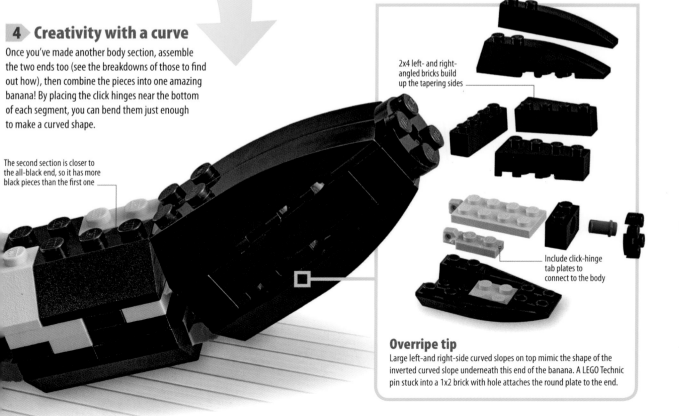

2x4 left- and right-angled bricks build up the tapering sides

Include click-hinge tab plates to connect to the body

Overripe tip

Large left-and right-side curved slopes on top mimic the shape of the inverted curved slope underneath this end of the banana. A LEGO Technic pin stuck into a 1x2 brick with hole attaches the round plate to the end.

Fruit and veg

Tech 4's further investigation reveals an entire larder full of colossal produce, enough for a minifigure space colony to live off for years! After building a banana, what other fruits or vegetables could you make?

WHAT'S NEXT

Fruit and vegetables come in all shapes and sizes, so chances are you will have LEGO pieces in your collection that can make something delicious.

APPLE

CHILI PEPPERS

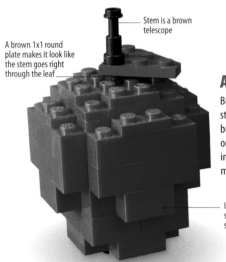

Stem is a brown telescope

A brown 1x1 round plate makes it look like the stem goes right through the leaf

Apple

Build a round object like an apple by starting with a circle at the base and building up, stepping your bricks outwards in the center and then back in again near the top. A leaf and stem make it easy to identify this fruit!

Use bricks for big, blocky shapes, and plates for small refinements

A LEGO Technic cross axle connects the stem to the pepper top

1x2 slope

Chili curve

Build a bend into your pepper model with a snap-together hinge that combines a 1x2 base and a 2x2 movable plate. A 1x2 slope fills in the gap between the two halves.

Most of this chili is made from 2x4 angled plates

1x2 plate and a 1x1 cone for the stem

A single-stud connection lets you attach the point at an angle

2x2 cone tip

Chilis

Watch out—these chili peppers are red hot! The challenge in building them is creating the bend in the middle. Assemble a simple chili out of angled plates, or use round pieces and a hinge for a more three-dimensional version.

PEAR

The stem is a 1x1 round brick and 1x1 slope attached to a 2x2 cone

A two-piece hinge makes the top crooked

Pair

Here's another way to build a rounded fruit! Unlike the traditionally constructed apple, this pear is built outwards from a central core of side-stud bricks.

Pairs for pears

Start with a core that alternates double plates between rows of four side-stud bricks. Stack plates to make the four-stud-wide front and back, and the two-stud-wide left and right sides.

Back-to-back 1x1 bricks with side studs point in opposite directions

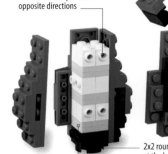

Place two 2x2 plates between each row of four side-stud bricks

2x2 round plate at the bottom

Mix dark pieces with light ones for a mottled look

MUSHROOMS

Mushrooms

There are lots of different ways to make mushrooms. Try using radar dishes or domes for the big round cap, and 1x1 round bricks or 2x2 round bricks for the narrower, cylinder-shaped stalk.

Textured round bricks add detail

Use a 2x2 dome for a smaller cap

ALL MY PRODUCE IS FRESHLY BUILT.

Substitute colorful pieces for a toadstool, or gray and black for a cooked mushroom!

CARROTS

4x16 wedge slope body

The last round brick is flipped around and connected by a LEGO Technic cross axle

Carrots

If you've got orange and green LEGO elements, you can probably make a pretty good carrot! Here are two different ways to do it, one using lots of pieces and the other just a handful. How will you build yours?

The root of it

Hold two long 4x16 wedges together by using short LEGO Technic cross axles to attach pairs of 2x2 round plates back-to-back, so that the studs stick out on both sides. The carrot top attaches to a 1x2 jumper plate on two 1x1 headlight bricks.

Carrot body is a stack of 2x2 round bricks, with a 2x2 cone for the pointy end

A gingerbread man

START HERE

Tech 4 has discovered a new alien being! Could this be the true ruling species of this world, not those scary "human" creatures? A gingerbread man is easier to build than it is to bake. Here's how to do it!

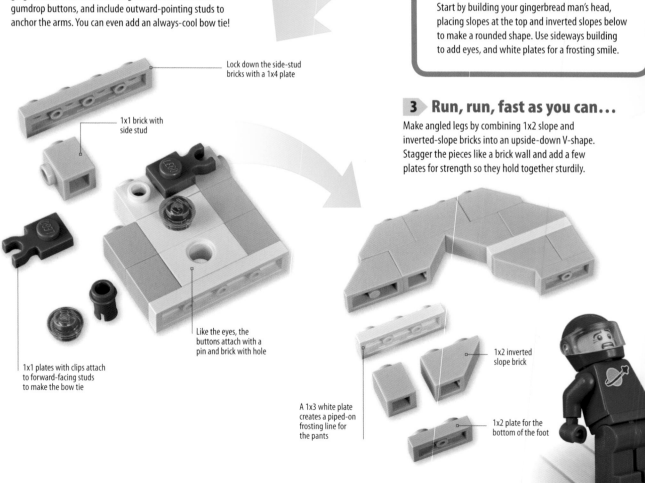

A 1x2 tile covers the top studs

Eyes are printed 1x1 round tiles attached to studded LEGO Technic pins set in 1x2 bricks with round holes

1 ⟩ A head above

Start by building your gingerbread man's head, placing slopes at the top and inverted slopes below to make a rounded shape. Use sideways building to add eyes, and white plates for a frosting smile.

2 ⟩ Fresh-baked body

Build the flat body out of tan or brown bricks for baked gingerbread, with white frosting details. Make a line of gumdrop buttons, and include outward-pointing studs to anchor the arms. You can even add an always-cool bow tie!

Lock down the side-stud bricks with a 1x4 plate

1x1 brick with side stud

Like the eyes, the buttons attach with a pin and brick with hole

1x1 plates with clips attach to forward-facing studs to make the bow tie

3 ⟩ Run, run, fast as you can...

Make angled legs by combining 1x2 slope and inverted-slope bricks into an upside-down V-shape. Stagger the pieces like a brick wall and add a few plates for strength so they hold together sturdily.

1x2 inverted slope brick

A 1x3 white plate creates a piped-on frosting line for the pants

1x2 plate for the bottom of the foot

4 ▸ Pop-off arms

Each arm is made out of a 1x2 brick, three 1x2 plates, and two 1x1 slopes. Attaching them to the body by just one stud makes it easy to snap them off—just like you might do with a real gingerbread man!

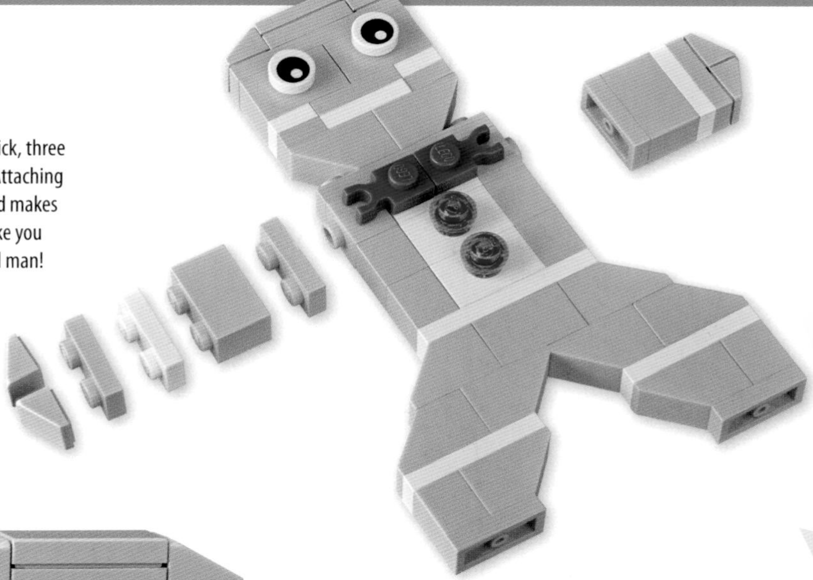

5 ▸ Ding! This batch is done

Your gingerbread man is complete! Now that you know how to build one, try making more gingerbread men and women with different designs of icing and candy decorations. Or you could just serve him up to your party guests...

I'M ALIVE! I'M ALIVE!

OH, CRUMBS.

A transparent plate looks like a jelly candy

A frosting belt locks the bricks together at the base

Make crumbs with a few 1x1 round plates

HALF-EATEN VIEW

More bakes

Deeper into the uncharted wilds of the pantry Tech 4 travels. There, hidden away inside of a gigantic jar labeled "Do Not Touch," he discovers a treasure trove that is almost as incredible…as it is edible!

WHAT'S NEXT?

You've already built one kind of dessert with your bricks. Now bake up a whole batch more! Try out these cookies and traybakes.

CUSTARD CREAM

COFFEE FUDGE BROWNIE

Custard cream

Build this sandwich cookie by assembling a pair of biscuits out of flat tan pieces, and using two white 2x2 jumper plates to make the custard-flavored filling in the middle.

Exposed studs mimic the traditional cookie's textured top

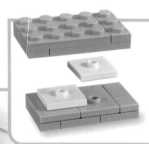

Jumper layer
The top layer of the bottom biscuit is covered with tiles and jumper plates so the filling pieces can sit in the center.

Upper biscuit made from two layers of plates

Coffee fudge brownie

Tiles for a smooth frosted top

Use plates of different shades of brown to make the fudge-filled brownie, and coat with a layer of tiles for coffee frosting.

Long and short plates lock the levels of the build together securely

For a different recipe, try nougat-colored pieces and make millionaire's shortbread!

WE ALL GO VERY WELL WITH A CUP OF TEA.

CHOCOLATE BISCUIT

Chocolate biscuit

This three-layered treat uses a simple combination of brown plates for the long chocolate biscuits, and dark brown plates for the chocolate buttercream filling squashed in between.

The order of the 1x6 and 2x6 plates alternates with each row

Since there aren't any 3x6 LEGO plates, you'll need to combine multiple six-stud-long pieces to get the right shape

CHOCOLATE SANDWICH COOKIE

Chocolate sandwich cookie

Two black 4x4 round plates are a perfect match for this snack's chocolate cookie top and bottom. A white 2x2 jumper plate in the center provides a single middle stud, so you can twist off the top part to get to the cream filling!

Hole connects to jumper plate's stud

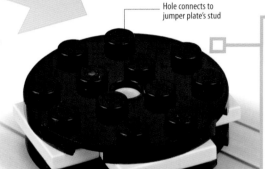

Cream filling

Place 1x2 tiles around the jumper plate to fill out this cookie's cream filling without blocking the twist-off function.

COOKIES

Cookies

Take four brown, tan, or nougat-colored corner plates and lock them together with a few plates on top to make chunky, lumpy homemade cookies. Pop on some 1x1 round plates or tiles for the chips!

Use multicolored pieces for rainbow chips, or black or brown for chocolate

Remove one or two plates for a bitten cookie

Cakes and pastries

Look at the LEGO pieces in your collection to decide what baked goods to build. Round pieces could become a Bakewell tart, or square pieces a Battenberg cake. If you have angled plates and hinges, you could even build a festive slice of birthday cake!

WHAT'S NEXT?

After trying out some flatter cookies and traybakes, try building up a batch of cakes. Use these sweet ideas to inspire you.

Lemon slice

Put together plates to make a rectangle of lemon-flavored cake with a sweet cream filling, and use yellow jumper plates to attach white tiles for diagonal stripes of frosting on top.

LEMON SLICE

Tiles on top hide the breaks between three yellow 1x2 jumper plates

The 1x3 tiles that form the frosting stripes are attached at an angle on the single studs of jumper plates.

Yellow 1x6 tiles for the outer edges

BATTENBERG CAKE

Studded surfaces give the cake a sugary texture

Each side is a 4x8 tan plate

Battenberg cake

Start this distinctively decorative cake by using yellow and pink tiles to build a checkered pattern on two 4x4 plates at the ends. A core covered with sideways-studded brackets lets you build the sides by attaching plates that face outwards in all directions.

If you don't have enough brackets to go inside the cake, you could build up the center as a stack of bricks instead.

Cherry Bakewells

To build a tasty tart, start with a round, brown base—you could construct it from bricks, or use a large half barrel to keep it simple. Add a layer or two of white pieces for the almond fondant, and attach a red LEGO Technic ball to the top for a candied cherry.

1x2 slopes for sloping edges

tart uses the same
es for its top as the
k-built one

Shortcrust pastry shell built from tan bricks and plates

A 4x4 radar dish fits on top of a half-barrel

The secret ingredient

Inside the half-barrel, a 2x2 round brick with a LEGO Technic cross axle pushed through its center hole forms a support column for a round radar dish.

Birthday cake

To make a slice of cake, arrange angled plates into a triangle for the frosted top, and then build a matching triangular base using hinged plates. Build up the sides and back, and attach the top portion. Add colorful decorations and don't forget a candle!

BIRTHDAY CAKE

Plug in a flame piece at the top

Flower element for a candle-holder

Use 1x1 plates with clips and rings for fancy frosting details

A white wall at the back for the cake's frosted edge

Make jelly-like layers of fruit filling with transparent colored round and square plates

Include multiple hinge plates for strength

Try different color bricks for different cake flavors, such as yellow for vanilla or brown for chocolate

Have a slice

Try narrow hinged plates at the tip of your cake slice, and wide-open ones at the back. The sides of the cake are constructed like brick walls, with layers of filling and frosting inside.

I THINK ONE SLICE WILL BE ENOUGH.

A popsicle

Tech 4 has found a portal to an ice region. Behind this heavy door is a labyrinth of frozen food. Cautiously, he unwraps something shaped like a spaceship and takes a bite. It's a delicious three-color popsicle!

START HERE

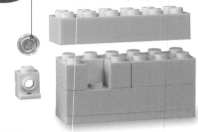

Transparent 1x1 round tile for ice—you could also use a round plate, or a colored piece for melting fruit juice

1 > An ice beginning

Start building your popsicle with the 2x6 bottom layer, its widest section. Bricks with side studs let you attach transparent pieces as tiny chunks of ice.

2 > Onward and upward

Next, switch colors and build the 2x4 middle section of the popsicle as a smaller wall of bricks, using slopes for an angled transition from the larger section beneath it. Place four 1x2 jumper plates at the top.

Recessed 1x1 headlight bricks make the ice sit close to the surface

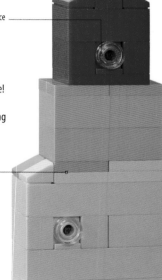

4 > A cool creation

Add a lollipop-style stick at the bottom, and your popsicle is complete! Try building the same design with different colors and patterns of melting ice. You could even make a patriotic version in the colors of a flag!

The colors of a real popsicle melt into each other, so mix in a few pieces in the middle section

3 > Tasty top

Change colors again for the 2x3 top section. The offset studs of the jumper plates underneath will center it on the middle section. Use 1x1 slopes and a 1x2 plate and tile to give it a rounded tip.

I HOPE THESE ARE AS COOL AS MY TUNES.

Stick-y situation

The popsicle stick is made by connecting three white cylinder-shaped LEGO Technic connectors together with black LEGO Technic connector pins. A pin with a cross-axle end at the top fits into the popsicle's base.

Frozen treats

What other desserts from the freezer can you make? With the right shapes and colors, you can combine your LEGO bricks to construct tall or flat ice-lollies, and even chocolate-covered ice-cream bars.

WHAT'S NEXT?

Some of the same techniques used to make a popsicle can be used for other kinds of frozen snacks, too.

SWIRLY SURPRISE

CHOCO BITE

STRAWBERRY DIP

1x2 tiles and a 2x2 radar dish attached to a 2x2 jumper plate on top

Leave off some brown pieces and add white slopes to make it look like someone has taken a bite!

Attach 1x1 round plates to bricks with side studs for candy bits

Stack tan 1x2 bricks for a wooden popsicle stick

Swirly surprise

Try a chilly challenge with the more complicated shape of a striped ice lolly. Make a cross-shaped stack of 2x4 bricks using two different colors. Alternate the colours in each stack to make stripes.

Choco bite

Build a simple chocolate ice cream bar by building a brick wall with slopes at the top. The rows of this one have alternating pairs of 2x2 and 2x3 bricks for strength.

Strawberry dip

Change up the colors and details on a simple ice cream bar for variety. This one has a top in a different color for a "dipped" look.

Use plates and tiles to build the ribbon

Curved half-arch pieces form a box-top bow

Gift note made from two angled plates

Room for dessert
The box's lining is built from black bricks and covered with smooth tiles. Tiles at the bottom of each compartment make the chocolates easy to remove.

Chocolate box
Once you've built up your chocolate treats, build compartments that are the perfect fit for them. Once you're done, build a box for them all with a removable lid. You could also add a bow and a gift note to the box to make it look extra fancy.

The box is built on a big 16x16 plate, but you could combine several smaller ones